Practical Know-how Flowers and Houseplants

SIMON &
SCHUSTER

LONDON • NEW YORK • SYDNEY • TORONTO

First published in Great Britain by
Simon & Schuster UK Ltd 2008
A CBS Company

ISBN 9 78184 737 2512

Simon and Schuster UK Ltd
Africa House
64–78 Kingsway
London WC2B 6AH

1 3 5 7 9 10 8 6 4 2

Design and illustrations by Jane Norman
Text by Jenny Kieldsen
Jacket design by Lizzie Gardiner
Printed and bound in China

Contents

Introduction

Flowers and houseplants add colour, interest
and a sense of well-being to your home.
It doesn't matter whether your indoor garden is
a fabulous conservatory or just a few pots on a
window-sill. If you care for your blooms you can
bring the outside in and lift your spirits
at the same time.

> **"** In all things of nature there is something of the marvellous. **"**
>
> *Aristotle, BC 385–322*

Easy Houseplants

Good examples

Don't be guided by large, showy plants in public
buildings; these are usually looked after by
professionals, and are often returned to the
nursery as soon as they are past their best.
Look around the homes of your friends to see
which plants flourish and grow well.

Busy Lizzie (impatiens)

These are really easy to grow (and propagate) and come in a fabulous range of colours, from hot pinks and reds to dark purples. Some species have very pretty variegated leaves too.

To keep plants bushy, pinch out the growing tips of young plants and prune mature plants each spring. The stems are succulent and brittle, and if you break one off and place it in water it will root easily. Feed during the growing season and water frequently in the summer.

"What's in a name?
That which we call a rose
By any other name would smell as sweet."

William Shakespeare, 1564–1616, Romeo and Juliet

"A rose is a rose is a rose."

Gertrude Stein, 1874–1946

African Violets (saintpaulia)

These can flower at any time of the year. They come in a wide variety of colours, though shades of purple are the most common. The flowers can have a single petal or several. They like bright light – ideally an east-facing window in the winter and a west-facing window in the summer. Be very careful when watering, not to get any water on the leaves, as this will make them go mouldy.

Spider Plants (chlorophytum)

So called because they produce tiny plantlets at the end of each stem. These hang down from the 'mother plant' and look like spiders. They're not too fussy about light (away from direct sun is best) and like to be watered liberally from spring to autumn. They are well suited to bathrooms.

" Every flower about a house certifies to the refinement of somebody. "

Robert G. Ingersoll, 1833–1899

Peace Lily (spathiphyllum)

These lilies have beautiful glossy, green, lance-shaped leaves. They produce white, cream or green flowers in the spring and summer. The flowers are usually fragrant smelling and will last for up to a week.

The lily needs to be kept out of direct sunlight, in a room that is draught free and warm in winter. The plant pot should stand on a tray of damp pebbles. Keep the compost moist in the summer and reduce watering in the winter.

❝Bread feeds the body, indeed, but flowers
feed also the soul.**❞**

The Koran

Pelargonium –
the correct name for Geraniums

One of the world's favourite houseplants, geraniums are very easy to grow and to propagate. They have a long flowering period and the clusters of blooms are available in a fantastic range of colours, with amazing new hybrids being created each year.

They will bloom for most of the year if kept on a sunny window-sill. Keep the compost rather dry (watering from below); over-watering is the main enemy of geraniums. 'Pinch back' young plants to encourage bushiness, do not re-pot until absolutely necessary, and remove any dead flowers and leaves as soon as possible.

Kangaroo Vine (cissus antarctica)

These plants cling with curly tendrils and will trail over a trellis or support. They are quite fast growing and have dark glossy green leaves. They like cool conditions with semi-shade or some good light, but not direct sunlight. Water well, from spring to autumn, and sparingly in the winter.

Mother-in-law's Tongue (sansevieria trifasciata laurentii)

If all else fails, this is the plant to try. It will grow in bright sunshine or shade, withstand draughts and periods without water and, rarely needs re-potting. The plant can, however, be killed by over watering in winter.

Suggestions for other easy houseplants:

begonias

tradescantia

philodendrons

ivies (hedera)

coleus

Growing citrus pips

This is good fun! You may not harvest your own oranges or lemons, but the stylish plants have shiny green leaves – and are free. Place two or three pips in a small pot (filled with compost) and just cover them over with a little more compost. Water well and put in a warm place. Cover with a piece of glass or tie a polythene bag around the pot until the seedlings appear. Make sure the glass or polythene doesn't touch the seedlings. If all of the pips sprout, transplant the strongest into separate pots.

Potting compost

Soil from the garden is unsuitable for all houseplants; it is likely to contain pests and diseases, which will flourish in the warmth of your home. Garden Centres carry a huge range of prepared nutrient-rich mixtures, and these are usually known as peat-based or soil-less composts.

Most compost contains a combination of peat, vermiculite or perlite. Damage to peat bogs has led to the peat being replaced by coir (coconut fibre), which is a sustainable product.

Highly specialised plants such as orchids seldom thrive unless the compost is exactly right. Most other plants are adaptable and will survive happily in a bought compost – with some feeding with a proprietary plant food during the summer months.

Nearly all houseplants like an acid compost and react badly to an excess of alkaline (chalk and lime). The main symptom of too much alkaline is yellow leaves.

" Aromatic plants bestow

no spicy fragrance while they grow;

but crushed or trodden to the ground, diffuse

their balmy sweets around."

Oliver Goldsmith, 1728–1774

Edible Flowers and Leaves

Growing herbs indoors

Buy pot-grown herbs from the garden centre to grow on your kitchen window-sill or in your cool conservatory. Pots of herbs bought in the supermarket won't last so long.

Six good herbs to buy:

parsley

thyme

lemon thyme

a small bay tree

coriander (an annual)

rosemary

All of these benefit from being outside in the summer, even if you don't have a garden. You can put them on an outside window-sill or in a window box or pot.

Basil (ocimum basilicum)

This herb is an exception to the rule as it's an annual, and you'll need to plant the seeds in pots in the springtime. Basil is very easy to propagate and you'll have lots of spare plants to give away to your friends. Nothing is better than fresh basil (especially with tomatoes). It also helps to deter flies in the kitchen.

❋

"The world is a rose;
smell it and pass it on to your friends."

Old Persian Proverb

If you have a window box

Try growing nasturtiums, marigolds, pansies and violas, all of which have edible flowers. Pull the petals from the marigold flowers and scatter them over cold puddings or salads. Wash flowers and leaves first and drain them well on kitchen paper.

❝Whatever a man's age, he can reduce it by
several years by putting a bright-coloured
flower in his buttonhole.**❞**

Mark Twain, 1835–1910

Flowers to eat

The flowers of any type of nasturtium or pansy may be eaten.

Nasturtiums

Both the flowers and leaves are edible. The leaves have a peppery flavour and are good in salads. The flowers can also go into salads, and can be used for decorating desserts. The petals are delicious in sandwiches with a little cream cheese.

Marigold (calendula officinalis)

This annual, which will seed itself naturally each year, is the only edible marigold.

Borage

These are very pretty small, bright blue flowers,
which look great floating in summer drinks.
They can also be frozen in ice cubes to add to
drinks such as gin and tonic.

✳

Elderflowers

The whole heads can be cooked with
gooseberries to give a wonderful Muscat flavour.

✳

Courgette flowers

These are the flowers that form before the
courgette itself. They are very delicate, and are
good dipped into a light batter and
quickly deep-fried.

✳

Rose petals

Red or pink look the best; dip them into lightly
beaten egg white, shake and then toss them in
caster sugar. Lay the petals on baking
parchment and leave until completely dry.
The rose petals make very pretty decorations
for puddings in the summer.

※

English Lavender

Incredibly versatile, lavender flowers should be
picked when in full bloom, but use only a small
amount in each recipe. Infuse a small handful in
hot milk, strain well, and use to make custards
or ice cream. Store the flowers in caster sugar
in a well-sealed jar. Use the sugar for baking,
leaving the flowers in if you wish. The flowers
look very pretty in a glass of champagne too.

※

Rose-scented geranium (pelargonium graveolens)

This plant has tiny indifferent flowers, but the leaves have a fantastic 'lemony' scent when crushed or brushed against. You can place 3–4 leaves (well washed) into the base of a cake tin before adding a Victoria sponge mixture. Peel the leaves from the cake when it is cool. Fill the sponge with lemon curd, if you like.

Dandelions

The young bright green leaves of dandelions are lovely in spring salads.

✳

Chillies (capsicum)

These plants are widely available now, and if you cook and use small fresh chillies, nothing is more pleasurable than 'snipping' a couple when you need them. They may be very hot, but removing the seeds helps to cool them down. They need some bright light and moist compost. If you don't harvest them all, they will drop on to the compost and root themselves into new plants, which can then be potted.

❝ *A kiss without a hug is like a flower without the fragrance.* **❞**

Maltese Proverb

❝ *Happiness held is the seed; happiness shared is the flower.* **❞**

Anon.

Sprouting seeds

You can either buy a special 'sprouter' or make your own by taking a large, wide-necked glass jar, a piece of nylon mesh cut from a pair of tights or stockings, and a large elastic band.

Put a dessertspoon of seeds into the jar and soak them in water for about 2 hours. Put the nylon mesh across the lid of the jar and secure with the elastic band. Turn upside down to drain the water and leave the jar propped at an angle. Rinse and drain the seeds twice daily until they sprout and grow.

Sprouting will take a few days, depending on the seeds and the warmth in your house, but as long as you rinse through with clean water, the seeds will sprout. It's very exciting!

Good seeds to sprout:

black and white mustard

coriander

cumin

fennel

fenugreek

lentils

alfalfa

chickpeas

" People from a planet without flowers
would think we must be mad with joy the
whole time to have such things about us. "

Iris Murdoch, 1919–1999

Cacti, Succulents and Bulbs

Easy care cacti

Contrary to popular belief, cacti are not difficult to care for, in fact they are fascinating plants and easy to care for. They can be grown from seed, but unless you are a very experienced gardener, buy them already growing.

Flowering cacti

Cacti will flower when they are mature, which is usually at two years old, and occasionally three. They need to receive as much bright sunlight as possible, and of course warmth. Most of the flowers are very beautiful and a great surprise when they appear. They need to be fed in the watering season, either with high potash or a proprietary cactus food. If possible, keep them in a cooler place in winter; an unheated bedroom would be perfect.

Potting compost

It should be light and well aerated, and made up of at least half gritty sand (not from the builder's yard as it's not suitable for plants!). This helps any surplus water drain away easily and quickly.

Watering - if in doubt, don't!

Only water once a fortnight, not on cold and damp days, and never leave cacti standing in water. Do not water at all from the beginning of October to the end of March.

Holiday friendly

Cacti are great plants to have if you are going on holiday, because they can be left without water for up to three weeks or more.

❋

" In the middle ages, people took potions for their ailments. In the 19th century they took snake oil. Citizens of today's shiny, technological age are too modern for that. They take extract of cactus instead. "

Enid Bagnold, 1889–1961

Re-potting

This does not need doing very often, as growth is slow, but if you need to re-pot – and the cacti are very prickly – hold a thick band of brown paper or newspaper around each plant.

Christmas/Easter flowering cactus (schlumbergera)

These plants produce a profusion of white or pinky-mauve flowers at either Christmas or Easter. They respond very well to used, damp teabags placed around the plant. Change these once a week and keep the soil moist, watering only from the bottom.

Aloe Vera (aloe barbadensis)

Break the leaves or spikes from an Aloe Vera plant and the sticky liquid that pours out can be rubbed straight on to your hands to soften the skin, or used to soothe a minor burn or sunburnt skin.

To propagate Aloe Vera

These plants make good gifts, and they are
easy to propagate as they take root quickly. Pull
off a spike or leaf, lay it against the inside of
a pot and fill the pot with compost.

❋

66 *Gardening is the purest of*
human pleasures. 99

Francis Bacon, 1561–1626

When to buy bulbs

They should be bought in August/September
and planted before the middle of October.
Go to a good garden centre, and make sure you
choose bulbs that are sold loose, checking that
they are firm and healthy looking.

*" In joy or sadness, flowers are
constant friends. "*

Kazuko Okakura, 1863–1913

Planting bulbs

Always use a proprietary bulb compost, and always plant the same named varieties of bulb in the same container, to help them flower together. All bulbs are happy to be close to each other in the bowl or pot, but not touching. If there is not a drainage hole in the bowl, put some broken 'crocks' in the bottom before filling with compost.

Hyacinths for Christmas

When planting bulbs in the house to flower at
Christmas, make sure you buy the 'prepared'
type, which are specially designed to flower
indoors. Blue hyacinths have the strongest
scent; buy early for the best choice.

Water the compost well, put in a black polythene
bag, and place in a cool, dark place until the
bulbs have sprouted about 5 cm (2 inches).
They will be very pale in colour. Bring them out
into the warmth of the house, and keep moist.
They should then flower in a few weeks' time.

Cut hyacinths

If the hyacinth flowers fall over – and they
sometimes do – cut them with as long a stem
as you can and put in a vase with water.
They will last just as long.

Crocuses

To get crocuses to flower in the house they
must be planted, as for all bulbs, in bowls or
pots then left outside.

✳

Keep an eye on them in the garden and, when
the buds appear, bring them indoors. They will
only flower a few days before the garden ones,
but are still a pleasure to have in the house.
Crocus bulbs are not available 'prepared'
as hyacinths are.

Narcissi and daffodils

These can also be planted outside in bowls or pots and brought in when the buds appear; species of miniature daffodils work well too. The best-scented narcissi varieties to plant are Paper White and Soleil d'Or (known as Sols).

Planting in the garden

All these bulbs can be planted in the garden afterwards; just leave the bowls outside after they have flowered and wait until all the leaves have died down. Remove the bulbs from the compost, then plant in the garden in the normal way. Hyacinths will revert from 'prepared' to normal.

"In the hope of the moon
Men fail to see the flowers
That blossom at their feet"

Albert Schweitzer, 1875–1965

❋

"Flowers are the sweetest things God ever
made and forgot to put a soul into."

Henry Ward Beecher, 1813–1887

" *Green fingers are the extension of a verdant heart.* **"**

Russell Page, 1906–1985

Plant Care

Minerals for plants

Save the water from boiling eggs for your plants, as it is full of minerals. Water from an aquarium or goldfish bowl is excellent too.

To water plants easily

A clean, well-rinsed washing-up liquid bottle
makes an ideal indoor watering can, enabling
you to control the water and avoid spilling
it on your furniture.

For healthy plants

It is really important to keep plants healthy.
Remove any fallen or discoloured leaves and
snip off flower heads as soon as they die.
Debris in the pot encourages mould.

To remove aphids

For green and white fly, and other nasty little
things that invade and make a sticky mess:
sprinkle a few spoonfuls of cold, soapy
washing-up water over the infested parts of
the plant. Repeat as necessary.

To keep large-leaved plants dust-free and clean

Rub the leaves with the inside of a banana skin
to help bring out the shine.

✳

Put the plant into the bath (or shower) and rinse
gently with warm water from the shower-head.
Leave the leaves to dry naturally.

✳

Gently wipe a little glycerine (from the chemist,
or with the baking ingredients in shops) over
the leaves using cotton wool.

Don't drown plants

Plant roots need air as well as water. Keeping the compost soaked all the time means death for most plants. It is usually best to put water into the tray at the bottom of the container rather than directly on to the topsoil.

"A morning glory at my window satisfies me more than the metaphysics of books."

Walt Whitman, 1819–1892

Too draughty or too warm

Plants don't like draughts or dry heat, so try
not to place them in the following positions:

between closed curtains and a window

❋

near an air-conditioning duct

❋

on a window-sill with a poor-fitting frame

❋

near or above a radiator

❋

too close to an open, gas or electric fire,
or a wood-burning stove

❋

in very bright sunlight or hot sun

Plants need daylight

They won't thrive in an unlit corner or a dark passageway.

Watering when you are on holiday

Lay an old towel in the bottom of the bath and stand your potted plants on it (without saucers). Fill the bath with 8–10 cm (3–4 inches) of water. So long as all your pots have holes in the bottom, the plants will automatically take up the water from the towel as they need it.

Pot bound?

This is how to recognise when a plant
is pot bound:

when the roots appear through the drainage hole.

the soil dries out very quickly between watering.

the stem and leaf growth seem very slow.

The final check: gently turn the pot upside
down, supporting the plant on your hand, and
ease it out of the pot with a twist. If it is pot
bound the roots will look matted and very
little soil will be visible.

Re-potting

Spring is the best time. Select a new pot, which is only slightly larger than the existing one, and quarter fill it with new compost. Water the compost well. Remove the plant from the existing pot and place it on top of the compost. Gradually fill in around it with compost, firming it down as you go. The plant stem should be at the same level as before. Tap the pot to settle the soil. Water carefully and place in the shade for a week.

" I always plucked a thistle
and planted a flower where I thought
a flower would grow.**"**

Abraham Lincoln, 1809–1865

Cut Flowers

Cutting tips

Always use sharp secateurs to cut flowers from your garden, and never cut flowers in the heat of the day. Either cut them in the morning, after the dew has gone, or in the late afternoon.

Flowers for the house

A rough guide to cutting flowers for the house is
that they should have stems long enough and
sturdy enough to hold the flower comfortably
in an arrangement.

*❝I'd rather have roses on my table than
diamonds at my neck.❞*

Emma Goldman, 1869–1940

Long-lasting blooms

Cosmos, Dahlias, and daisy type blooms will often last the longest. Make sure the flowers are completely open and that you remove all the leaves below the vase waterline, because they go mouldy very quickly if left in water.

Cutting roses and
herbaceous flowers:

When cutting roses from your garden for the house, cut as if you were pruning – in other words at an angle to an outward-facing bud.

❋

66 *Flowers are restful to look at. They have neither emotions nor conflicts.* 99

Sigmund Freud, 1856–1939

Large bunches

Large bunches of any type of flowers enjoy
sitting in a deep bucket filled with cold water (in
a cool place) for an hour or so before you
arrange them in the house.

Bought flowers from the florist or supermarket

It is a good idea to cut 2.5 cm (1 inch) from the
bottom of the stems, then leave them to soak
in cold water for an hour or so before arranging.
A diagonal cut is best as this gives the
flowers the opportunity to take up
as much water as possible.

Sweet Peas

Cut sweet peas with stems as long as you can. Put them in a simple glass vase and enjoy their heady scents. To get sweet peas that smell, check on the seed packet to see whether they are scented or not. Sometimes, the more frilly the bloom the less scented the flower.

" *I like flowers, I also like children, but I do not chop their heads and keep them in bowls of water around the house.* **"**

George Bernard Shaw, 1856–1950

" *Where flowers bloom so does hope.* **"**

Lady Bird Johnson, 1912–2007

Damaged flowers

Beware of flowers that are outside the florist or garage and are tainted with car exhaust fumes. Check that there are no fading leaves and that the flowers look fresh. If flowers are for an important occasion, it is worth phoning the florist to check which day they get a fresh delivery.

Supermarket and garage Flowers

These are sometimes worth buying, but as they are kept in such hot surroundings they don't last for long. Try to go to a florist, where it is always cool, and the flowers are kept in the best conditions.

❝ *To be overcome by the fragrance of flowers is a delectable form of defeat.* **❞**

Beverly Nichols, 1898–1983

✳

❝ *When sending flowers through the post, wrap well in damp newspaper and dip the ends in melted wax.* **❞**

Mrs Beeton, 1836–1865

> **❝** A flowerless room is a soulless room, to my way of thinking; but even one solitary little vase of a living flower may redeem it. **❞**

Vita Sackville-West, 1892–1926

Flower Arranging

Colourful foam

There is a huge range of colours and shapes of
florists' foam available, if you buy it in a block
use a serrated knife to cut to the
size you want.

Basic flower arranging equipment:

Floral foam, florists' foam or similar

❋

Waterproof tape to hold the foam in place,
available in three colours – white,
green and clear.

❋

Floral stem tape, strong and stretchable to
lengthen and strengthen stems.

❋

Sharp secateurs, or a sharp knife

❋

Waterproof clay – use this like glue to position
candles or figures in an arrangement.

Contain it

Remember that any container can be used as a vase – be creative and daring!

Start with the largest

Arrange large flowers first, and get the balance right before popping in smaller flowers and greenery to fill the gaps. As a general rule flowers should be twice the height of the container they are in.

To revive wilting flowers in a vase

Snip off about 2.5 cm (1 inch) from the ends, remove any dead leaves and then return the flowers to a washed vase of cold water.

Sugar to perk up flowers

If you don't have any flower food to put with cut
flowers, a tablespoon of granulated sugar will
work just as well.

Herbal foliage

Woody, long-stemmed herbs such as rosemary
and bay make good background greenery in a
mixed arrangement. They'll also provide
a lovely scent.

To keep tulips upright

Make a hole by sticking a pin right through the
top of the stem, just below the flower head.
This really does work!

Preventing pollen stains

The long stemmed lilies (*Lilium* Star Gazer) with huge flowers and a beautiful scent do have a disadvantage: the orange/yellow pollen can stain clothes if you brush against the flowers. There are two remedies here: either snip the stamens out of the lilies when you are arranging them. Alternatively, it is quite easy to remove the pollen by lifting it off with a piece of sticky tape, then washing the garment in the normal way.

A cautionary note

Be careful if you have pets! If a cat or other household pet brushes against lily pollen then ingests it through licking its fur, the consequences can be fatal.

Don't put them together

Daffodils and tulips won't work in arrangements
with other flowers as the sticky toxic secretions
from their stems will kill the other flowers. They
are rarely in flower at the same time, but they
can be arranged together if you wish.

Twice as good

If you stand your flower arrangement in front of
a mirror (on a mantelpiece, chest of drawers or
hall table), it will seem as though it contains
twice as many flowers, as well as making
twice the impact.

To keep flowers upright in an arrangement

Plastic hair-rollers are really good if you have any: stand them upright in the bottom of the vase. Support the flower stems in the rollers. Don't use a see-through container though!

Flowers that are too short

If the stems are too short for your vase,
support them in plastic drinking straws, then
cut these to length to fit the vase.

To make woody-stemmed
flowers last longer

Roses and other flowers with a woody stem last
longer in water when leaves low down
the stem are trimmed off.

Alternative florists' foam

If you don't have any florists' foam for a flower arrangement, you could try a criss-cross of sticky tape over the top of the vase, finishing with a piece around the rim to secure the edges. Stand the flowers in the squares to hold them upright. Don't fill the vase too full with water though.

Keeping containers clean

Make sure that all flower vases, baskets and any other containers are kept scrupulously clean, as bacteria from a previous arrangement can contaminate a new one.

For a wedding

If it's a summer wedding, you could tie sprigs
of lavender or rosemary to the napkins, with
matching ribbon. Small potted plants also look
good on the table and can be planted
outside later.

An old wives' tale

It is said that putting foxgloves into a flower
arrangement will make all of the
flowers last longer!

Christmas table arrangement

Ivy leaves artfully arranged on a white tablecloth,
or stuck to a red ribbon to wrap around white
napkins, makes the table look festive.

＊

"*Love is the only flower that grows and
blossoms without the aid of seasons.***"**

Kahil Gibran, 1883–1931

A posy for the table

In summer, a simple posy of garden flowers in a jam jar looks pretty on a window-sill or the table for lunch or tea. Pick them on the day – it doesn't matter if they don't last long. If your child has picked flowers for you, it is really important to put them in water first – and then to reiterate that it's best not to pick flowers in the wild, particularly if they're wild bluebells!

To clean a glass or cut-glass vase

Fill the vase with warm water and add one or two denture cleaning tablets (depending on the size). Leave to soak overnight then wash and rinse thoroughly.

"*I perhaps owe having become a painter to flowers.*"

Claude Monet, 1840–1926

" There are always flowers for those who want to see them. "

Henri Matisse, 1869–1954

Dried Flowers

Where to grow

Most flowers that are gathered for drying are
better grown in full sun. Pick them in the
morning, after any dew has evaporated, and
obviously not on a wet day.

When to pick them

Try to pick the flowers when they are not quite
fully in bloom; they will continue to open after
being picked. Double check that each bloom is
perfect and give a shake to remove
any insects.

Grouping them

Group flowers together in varieties, remove any
leaves, put into bundles and secure each
one with a rubber band.

Suggested flowers to dry:

hydrangeas

delphiniums

strawflowers/everlasting (helichrysum)

statice

yarrow (achilliea)

poppy seed heads (papaver)

globe thistle (echinopsis ritro)

love-in-a-mist seed heads (Nigella)

Chinese lantern (physalis)

honesty (lunaria)

lavender and sea lavender

South African daisy (helichrysum)

tall wild grasses

" There was once a Dormouse
who lived in a bed
Of delphiniums (blue) and geraniums (red)
And all the day long, he'd a wonderful view
Of geraniums (red) and Delphiniums (blue). "

A.A. Milne, 1882–1956

Keep in a cool, dry place

The most important aspect of drying flowers is to keep them in the dark. Remove them from the sunlight as soon as possible as this helps to keep the colours bright and natural looking.

✺

A good place for dried flowers is an attic, dark garage or shed – or even an under-stairs cupboard. The area needs to be cool, airy and not at all damp.

✺

" Plant the garden of your life with friendship's lovely flowers. "

Anon.

" 'Twas a very small garden;
The paths were of stone,
Scattered with leaves,
With moss overgrown. "

Walter de la Mare, 1873–1956

Hanging

Hang the bundles of flowers upside-down to dry. This keeps the stems straight and the flower heads upright. Use wire or string, attached to rubber bands, and hang the flowers from hooks or a convenient beam.

Drying time

This depends on many factors, but you're looking for a dry and stiff flower, not a limp and damp one.

Flower heads

If you are only drying flower heads, they can be put out on newspaper and kept in the same dark, airy conditions.

A collection from nature

Keep an eye open for interesting twigs, cones, rushes, and even nuts, when you're out for a country walk. Look out for sea lavender when you're by the sea as this dries particularly well.

Dried flower arrangement

Dried flowers look good in baskets of any size.
You can use either florists' wire mesh or foam
(not soaked in water) to keep the flowers in
place. Cover the foam with some dry moss and
then build up your arrangement. For other foams,
specifically for dried flowers, see page 92.

Cutting dried flowers

Always cut dried flowers with a sharp knife or
scissors; ragged edges are not good
for arrangements.

Moss and foam

Sphagnum Moss, used to cover the surface of dried flower arrangements, is available in florists. Look on the internet for preserved moss, known as Finland Moss.

Dry foam (non-porous) is available specifically for arranging dried flowers. Desert Foam is also used for dried flowers. It is non-porous and easier to use for delicate stems.

Away from the heat

When they are arranged, keep out of direct sunlight and away from radiators, fires or fan heaters, to minimize fading.

Dried Flowers

Lavender bags

Pick the lavender when the flowers are open to
their fullest, lay the stems on newspaper and
leave until completely dry. Rub the flowers from
the stems and use to fill little bags.

To make the bags

Cut pretty cotton material into circles (approx.
15 cm/6 inches in diameter) with pinking
shears. Add some lavender and tie up tightly
with some matching ribbon, leaving long tails if
they are to be hung in the wardrobe.

Storing dried flowers:

All dried flowers need to be handled very carefully. Wrap them in newspaper and place in a cardboard box. The box should be stored in a dry place, such as a garage or shed. The cold will not be a problem, but watch out for small rodents and insects.

"True friendship is like a rose: we don't realise its beauty until it fades."

Evelyn Watson, 1921–1950

To make a small gift using dried flowers

Group some matching flowers and grasses, tie each arrangement tightly with string, then snip the stalks to an even length. Wrap some coloured ribbon around to disguise the string and tie into a pretty bow.

" *But, O young beauty of the woods,*
Whom nature courts with fruits and flowers,
Gather the flowers but spare the buds. "

Andrew Marvell, 1621–1678